Extreme Sports

Contents

In-Line Skating **2**

Skydive **10**

Snowboarding **18**

You've Got to Spin to Win **26**

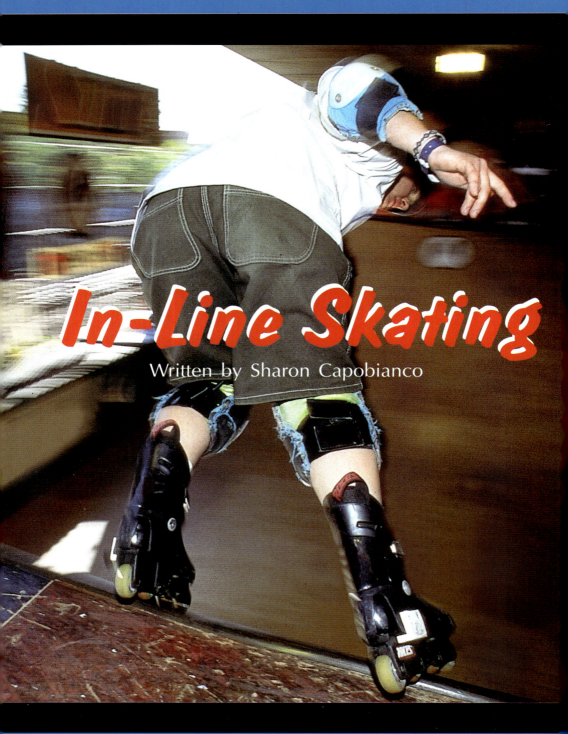

In-Line Skating

Written by Sharon Capobianco

Summer in the Early 1700s: Roller Skates Are Made

Joseph Merlin is missing his winter sport of ice-skating. He nails wooden spools to strips of wood and puts them on his shoes. The first pair of quad skates, or roller skates, is made!

1832: The "Rolito" Arrives

Robert Tyers invents a five-wheel in-line skate (*but* stops and turns are nearly impossible).

1980: "Rollerblades" Hit the Street

Ice hockey players Scott and Brennan Olson redesign the in-line skate, and the Rollerblade craze begins.

Today

In-line skaters compete in events that call for
speed,
balance,
and nerves of steel.

Aggressive Skating

Aggressive skating began as off-season training for ice hockey players. Aggressive in-line skaters do many stunts. They jump over things; do flips; ride stairs, walls, and ramps. Some aggressive in-line skating is done in the streets. This is called street skating. Another type of in-line skating is done at in-line skating parks specially made for skating. These parks have half-pipes and pools.

Downhill In-Line Skating

In-line racing has taken place since 1989, but competitive downhill in-line skating events took place first at the eXtreme Games of 1995. Downhill in-line skaters go down courses that have been chosen for their turns and slope. Competitors try to get through the course quicker than the other skaters. Skaters use special skates that will absorb the bumps and rough roads.

In-Line Talk

In-line skaters have a language all of their own!

Black Ice
A smooth recently paved street.

Drafting
Skating closely behind another skater in the air pocket that's created.

A Flyer
A skater who charges ahead of a large pack of skaters.

Half-pipe
A skating surface that looks like a pipe that has been cut longwise down the middle.

What other sports make use of air pockets?

Hook
When a skater gets in the way of a skater who is trying to pass.

Pool
A skating surface that looks like an empty swimming pool.

Session
A period of skating.

Vert
"Vertical" skating, usually done in a half-pipe or pool.

In-line skaters need protective gear. Injuries can happen a lot, especially among the aggressive skaters. Helmets, extra-large knee pads, elbow pads, wrist and shin guards are the skateboarder's smart wear.

Skydive

**Retold by Mark Iversen
for Annie Miles**

Hi! Annie Miles, skydiver, here! I don't know why, but one day, I decided that it might be fun to jump out of a plane. It was a strange decision for me to make because, like a lot of people, I am scared of heights. I did a bungee jump once and went away thinking that I would never do anything like that again! So, on the way to the airfield on the day of the jump, I had mixed feelings of both excitement and fear.

What You Need to Know:

Even when you jump with an instructor, you need to know how to make your jump. You need to know:

How to get out of the plane
You have to sit on the sill of the door. Your feet must be tucked under the plane.

How to free-fall
You have to spread your arms and legs out to the side. Your back needs to be arched backward with your head and eyes looking back.

How to land
When you and the instructor land, the instructor's feet need to hit the ground first. You need to tuck your knees up to your chest and then slide on your rear.

We tried these things on the ground, but I was feeling scared. I was afraid that when it came time to jump out of the plane, I would not be able to get my body into the right position.

When it did come time to do the jump, I collapsed like ice cream melting in the sun. The plane ride was cramped. On board were the jumpers, the instructors, and all the gear. The view from the plane was amazing. We were flying over farmland, and I could see the ocean in the distance. I asked a lot of questions; I was trying to reassure myself that these people knew what they were doing and that I was going to be OK.

When we reached the height that we were going to jump from, the plastic door cover was rolled up. The calm and quiet of the plane was replaced by the sound of rushing wind. I began to feel scared and nervous again.

My instructor and I were going first. We shuffled over to the door. I told myself not to hold on to anything, as I may not let it go. I sat on the sill of the door. It was not as hard as I thought, because the instructor's weight on my back was balancing me. I closed my eyes and, in no time, we were out in the air.

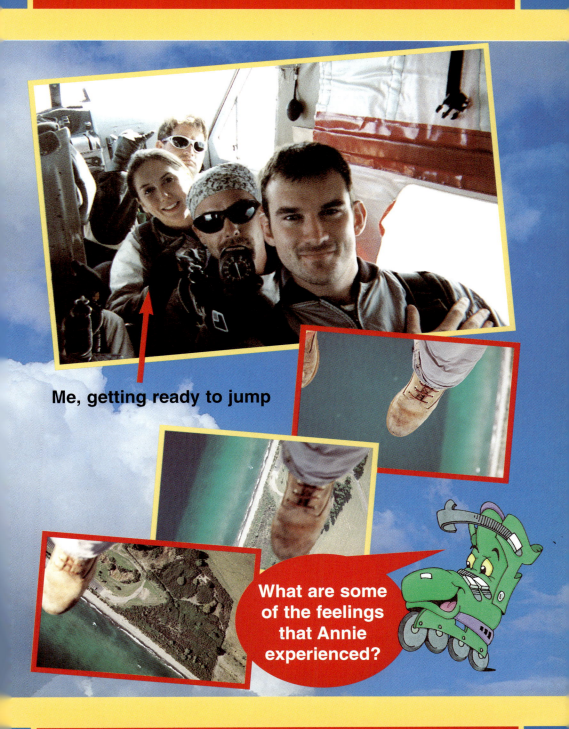

To my surprise, my body moved itself into the free-falling position easily. I opened my eyes and began to look around. The view was breathtaking. The feeling was great. The wind was rushing around me. I had this strong feeling of freedom. It seemed like we were falling in slow motion, but it was only fifty seconds until the instructor pulled the cord that opened the parachute. I didn't even have time to think about it *not* opening.

Free-falling

With the parachute opened, it seemed like we were floating upward. My feelings of fear were replaced with excitement. I began to scream with delight. Then we were floating at a slower pace, down to the ground. Now that the jump was nearing the end, I had to think about getting into the landing position. I tucked my knees up as my instructor's feet hit the ground and then we both slid onto our rears. The ground felt great, but already my mind was thinking about my next skydive.

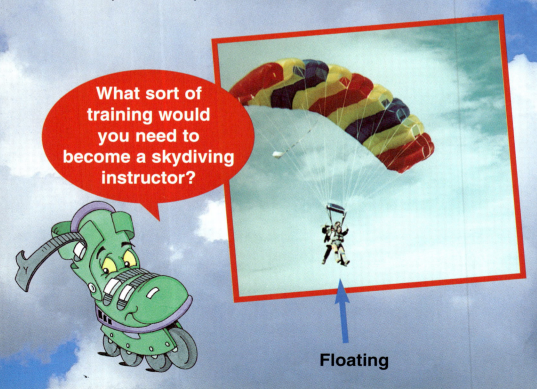

What sort of training would you need to become a skydiving instructor?

Floating

Snowboarding

Written by Paul Reeder

Snowboarding is not a new idea.

1929

Jack Burchett talks about surfing the snow. He cuts out a piece of wood and ties it to his feet with a rein from a horse's bridle and some clothesline.

1965

Sherman Poppen makes a way for his children to surf the snow near their home in Michigan. He puts together a pair of children's skis and invents something that looks like a sled. He calls it the Snurfer. He then builds more Snurfers to sell to other people.

Now

Many people have worked – and still work – to make snowboards better and faster. Snowboard competitors push for more events that challenge their snowboarding skills.

The Winter Olympics

The Winter Olympics in Nagano, Japan, was the first Olympics to hold snowboarding events. Olympic snowboarders competed for the gold in two events: the Alpine Giant Slalom and the Freestyle Competition.

Which other sports have slalom events?

Alpine Giant Slalom Events

In Alpine Giant Slalom events, snowboarders speed downhill through a series of gates. They go as fast as they can. If they miss a gate, the chance for the gold is lost.

Freestyle Events

In Freestyle events, competitors perform tricks as they snowboard down U-shaped channels of snow called half-pipes. Competitors can include their own choices of tricks in their performances. Points are given to snowboarders for

- How high they go

- How well they land

- How well they perform tricks that involve rotations (spins and flips)

- Including tricks of great difficulty (and performing them well)

- Including a wide variety of tricks (and performing them well)

The Tricks of the Snowboarder

Anyone can learn the tricks of snowboarding. And learning tricks is fun. Every day on the snow brings new excitement, especially when each time a trick is tried, things turn out differently.

What are some tricks that snowboarders can do?

YOU'VE GOT TO

Spin to Win

Written by
Kerrie Capobianco

Your heart is thumping. You are ready to jump – to free-fall into the air with only a rubber cord around your legs. You twist, you turn, you spin, you flip.

Then your jump is all over. Your heartbeat goes back to normal, but the excitement and thrill are still with you. This is the sport of bungee jumping.

The First Bungee Jumpers

Legends of the South Pacific tell of a woman who tied vines to her ankles and jumped from a tree to flee from her unkind husband. The people of her village tried to copy her jump. They jumped from high wooden towers with vines tied to their ankles. They believed that if they did this, it would show how brave they were and that it would bring a good harvest.

Today

Bungee jumpers all over the world plunge headfirst to earth.

Competitive Bungee Jumping

The earliest international bungee-jumping competitions took place in the United States at the first eXtreme Games held in Providence, Rhode Island, in 1995.

In competitive bungee jumping, each competitor is weighed before the jump. This is to make sure the right bungee cord is used. There are five different cords to choose from. All of the bungee cords are made of latex. The cords will stretch to over 150 feet (about 45 m) under the stress of the jumper's weight. That is why it is important to make sure that a jumper is weighed and the right cord is used.

After the right cord has been chosen, the jumper takes an elevator to the top of the jump site. A jumpmaster waits at the top.

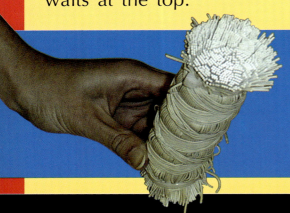

The bungee cord is made up of lots of long latex bands that are held together.

One end of the cord is tied to the platform off which the jumper will dive. The other end is tied to the jumper's ankles by a special harness. The jumper is now ready to dive off the platform. At the bottom of the platform, a crew waits to help the jumper out of the harness.

They wait and watch as the competitors somersault and twist as they fall through the air, spinning to win.

Index

aggressive skating 5
Alpine Giant Slalom 20–21

black ice 8
bungee cords 30–31
bungee jumping 10, 27–31
    competitive 30–31

downhill in-line skating 6–7
drafting 8

eXtreme Games 6, 30

floating 16
flyer 8
free-falling 11, 14
Freestyle events (snowboarding)
    20, 22, 23

half-pipes 4–5, 8, 23
hook 9

in-line skating 2–9
    aggressive 5
    downhill 6–7

landing (after skydiving) 16–17

parachute 14, 16
pools 4–5, 9
protective gear, in-line skaters 9

"Rolito" 3
Rollerblades 3
rollerskates 3

session 9
skydiving 10–17
snowboarding 18–25
    Olympic events 20
    tricks 24–25
Snurfer 19
street skating 5

vert 9

Winter Olympics 20